OH NO, MY MOM HAS T

Author: Rodricka Y. Brice-Curry

Illustrator: Maria Malyutina

This book is dedicated to my son, Cameron James Curry and to all the military children across the world. Being a military child is not easy. Deployments are tough on both the child and parent. Sometimes we will not be able to be there for all our child/children's special days and events while serving our country. Some of the most wonderful and independent children are raised from military families.

Oh no, my mom has to go!

She is deploying!

She will be leaving dad and I in five days.

My mom and dad work for the Air Force!
My mom's job is to help sick people feel better.

When I am sick, she is my doctor.
She checks my temperature, gives me kisses
and grants all my wishes.
I am going to miss my mom.

My mom and I went to sit outside on the porch together.

My friend yells from the street, "Hey Cameron, come play!"

I am just not in the mood today.

"Mom I do not want you to leave,

can you please stay with me?"

She picks me up and squeezes me tight.

Mom say, "I promise to be back as soon as I can."

"While I am gone, I need you to be strong and be our helping hand."

As it gets dark, mom carries me

into the house to prepare for bed.

She lays me in my bed.

She starts to search for something high in the closet.

Mom pulls out her camera and takes a picture of us together.

She says, "picture are memories to keep,

so that is what will do this week!"

Take lots and lots of pictures.

She hums me a song, until I fell asleep.

It is morning already, only 4 days to go!

We have to get up, we cannot move slow.

I jump in the bed with mom and dad

so they can wake up.

Mom says, "be our big helper by brushing your teeth."

I walk to the bathroom and push my stool to the sink.

Daddy turns the water on, so we can brush together.

Flash, flash, is all we see.

There is mommy taking pictures of me.

Dad ask us to get dress, he has a surprise.

We put cloths on and get in the car.

"Are we traveling far?" mom says.

We pull up to the mall, her favorite place.

Mom and I both have big smiles on our face.

We follow mom in a few stores to look for shoes.

"Cameron, now it's your turn to get something new,"

as we walk into the toy store.

I see my favorite toy, an airplane!

I shout "airplane, airplane, airplane!"

I start to run away to grab it.

"No no no, come hold our hand" mom said.

"Be our big helper by walking close

and not running off again."

I grab their hands, as dad buys my toy.

She takes a picture of us.

We made it home and it is time for my bath.

My dad runs the water and mom helps me undress.

"Splash, splash" I jump in and water goes everywhere.

Mom laughs and grabs a cup to wash my hair.

After taking a bath, dad dries me off with a towel.

I run to my room to pick out my night pajamas.

"Mom look at me!"

"I am being a big helper" shouting with glee.

She smiles, gives me a thumbs up and tucks me into bed.

"Let's take a picture of this moment" and kisses me on the head.

Only 3 more days, with mommy before she leaves.

I smell something good coming from the kitchen.

I hop out the bed and see daddy cooking.

"Morning son, come be my helper in cooking mommy's breakfast."

He cracks three eggs and I help him mix.

Dad and I cook pancakes, eggs, bacon, and grits.

We carry the food to mom's room.

Dad leans in close and kisses mom on the head.

She said, "let's take a picture of our great breakfast in bed."

Oh no, daddy and I made a mess in the kitchen.

I saw daddy and mommy cleaning, then came the singing.

Mom and I love singing the cleanup song as we put things away.

I grab the broom to help sweep the floors.

Mom said "let me get this picture, of our big helper doing chores!"

That evening, Mommy got some bags to start packing her cloths.

I ran to my room to grab my teddy bear.

I brought it back to mom, "take this with you."

"Hold this tight when you sleep at night" I said.

"Thank you, Cameron you're so sweet" mom said.

"I promise to call you every night, until I get on my return flight."

I gave her a hug and dad snaps a picture.

The next day mom says, "I have an idea, let's have a paint party!"

We ran to her craft room, to grab some stuff.

Red, white and blue were the colors I used.

The same colors of our flag, that my parents salute too.

We took lots of family pictures, as the sun started to set.

My heart was filling with good memories as we laid.

Cuddling up with my mom, this is where I want to stay.

Oh no, this is the last day before mommy has to go!

That afternoon, dad droves us to the park to have some fun.

I love going to the park, it is where I can slide and run.

Mom said she needs help counting the kids by the swing.

I count "1, 2, 3, 4, 5, 6, 7 and 8."

"Great, be our big helper and take eight popsicles to share!"

Dad and I carry them, arms waving in the air.

She takes a picture.

As we get back home, I'm started to feel sad again.

I crawl into my mom's arms, dad sits down too.

We are both going to miss mom very much.

From her soft kisses, good cooking, to her loving touch.

She reads me some stories out loud and rocks me to sleep.

Dad takes our picture.

The next morning, we are off to an early start.

We get to the airport and dad grabs her bags out the car.

Mom picks me up and carries me all the way to her gate.

She said, "I have a gift for you, son" and pulls out a picture book.

"These are all the pictures of us this week."

Mom said "I will keep your teddy bear and you will keep these pictures of me. Look at the pictures, every night before you go to sleep."

She gives dad and I tons of hugs and kisses filled with love.

As she walks away, she turns around to say,

"be daddy's big helper every day!"

We shout, "see you later mommy."

I do trust we will be together again!

I am just going to miss her, she is my best friend.

I love you mommy!

The End

CPSIA information can be obtained
at www.ICGtesting.com
Printed in the USA
LVRC091931051121
702556LV00003B/64